Good Habits

By Alan Searing Based upon his mp3 CD

Available at http://bit.ly/w6fLRh

Disclaimer

This e-book has been written to provide information about its topic. Every effort has been made to make this eBook as complete and accurate as possible. However, there may be mistakes in typography or content. Also, this e-book provides information only up to the publishing date. Therefore, this eBook should be used as a guide – not as the ultimate source.

The purpose of this eBook is to inform and educate. The author and the publisher do not warrant that the information contained in this e-book is fully complete and shall not be responsible for any errors or omissions. The author and publisher shall have neither liability nor responsibility to any person or entity with respect to any loss or damage caused or alleged to be caused directly or indirectly by this e-book.

The author and publisher have used their best efforts in preparing this e-book. The author and publisher make no representation or warranties with respect to the accuracy, applicability, fitness, or completeness of the contents of this report. The information contained in this report is strictly for educational purposes.

Copyright 2012 and Published by Solutions4U Hoddesdon EN11 8DN UK

Contents

Page

	Introduction	4
1.	Eat an Apple a Day	5
2.	Smile at strangers	6
3.	Watch Your 'self-talk'	8
4.	Repeat your own Affirmations daily	10
5.	Never be late	12
6.	Choose your company carefully – mix with the right people	14
7.	Laugh at yourself	16
8.	Breathe deeply three times a day for three minutes	19
9.	Walk for One Mile three times a week	23
10.	Live in 'the Now' this very minute	25
11.	Remember the past is the past	27
12.	Believe in Yourself	32
13.	Visualize Your Goals daily	33
14.	Play a CD instead of listening to the radio	35
15.	Read motivational/inspirational books every day	37
16.	Go the Extra mile	38
17.	Act as if you are at where you wish to be	43
18.	Tell your partner or a family member you Love them	44
19.	Carry out random acts of kindness for strangers	46
20.	Watch One hour less television every day	47
21.	Be courteous to all	50
	Conclusion	52
	Resources	53

Introduction

Habit

I am your constant companion
I am your greatest helper or your heaviest burden
I will push you onward or drag you down to failure
I am completely at your command
Half the things you do, you might just as well turn them over to me,
and I will be able to do them quickly and correctly
I am easily managed; you must be firm with me
Show me exactly how you want something done, and after a
few lessons I will do it automatically
I am the servant of all great men
And, alas, of all failures as well
Those who are great, I have made great
Those who are failures, I have made failures
I am not a machine, though I work with all the precision
of a machine. Plus, the intelligence of a man
You may run me for profit, or run me for ruin; it makes no
difference to me.
Take me, train me, be firm with me and I will put the world
at your feet
Who am I?

I am a HABIT!

Author Unknown

1. Eat an Apple a Day

Why?
What difference does it make?
What if it's true that an apple a day keeps the doctor away?

Many of us forget that sometimes, the simplest answers are the best. Better health could be as easy as reaching for the fruit bowl for some apples next time you need a snack

In 2004, USDA scientists investigated over 100 foods to measure their antioxidant concentration per serving size. Two apples—Red Delicious and Granny Smith—ranked 12th and 13th respectively. Antioxidants are disease-fighting compounds. Scientists believe these compounds help prevent and repair oxidation damage that happens during normal cell activity. Apples are also full of a fibre called pectin—a medium-sized apple contains about 4 grams of fibre. Pectin is classed as a soluble, fermentable and viscous fibre, a combination that gives it a huge list of health benefits.

An apple won't replace your toothbrush, but biting and chewing an apple stimulates the production of saliva in your mouth, reducing tooth decay by lowering the levels of bacteria.

Some health benefits of eating apples

The soluble fibre found in apples binds with fats in the intestine, which translates into lower cholesterol levels and a healthier you.

Research has found that eating apples can help prevent a whole range of medical conditions;
e.g. Alzheimer's, Parkinson's, Gallstones, diarrhea and constipation
Also you can get a healthier heart.

So is it not worthwhile at least considering eating an Apple a Day? As Jim Rohn said "it's easy to do and it's also easy not to do" so why not take the easy to do route and get the benefits of eating an apple a day?

2. Smile at strangers

Don't you think you feel much better when you receive a smile from a friend or loved one?
A smile is something that costs nothing to give and yet creates good feelings with those who receive one.

Smile--Smile--Smile a poem by Lealon R. Tate

A smile is beautiful with all its charm
Something to give but does no harm
A smile is a frown only upside down
It has a good feeling, just look around
A smile is a flash that cannot be sold
It has everlasting pleasure we are told
A smile is like the sunshine at its very best
Some wear it all the time until they lay down to rest
A smile is valuable like silver and gold
But it cannot be bought just always on hold
A smile is nothing till someone gives it away
Just try your best to receive it someday
A smile is like a statue that enriches the mind
You cannot steal or throw away but not hard to find
A smile is for the rich also for the poor
The benefits are the same till there is no more
A smile is for everyone with its action so true
It creates happiness in the home for me and you
A smile is a smile as known to mankind
Stand up in front and smile not stand behind.

And here are some more reasons to smile

From Mark Stibich, Ph.D., former About.com Guide

1. Smiling Makes Us Attractive

We are drawn to people who smile. There is an attraction factor. We want to know a smiling person and figure out what is so good. Frowns, scowls and grimaces all push people away -- but a smile draws them in

2. Smiling Changes Our Mood
Next time you are feeling down, try putting on a smile. There's a good chance you mood will change for the better. Smiling can trick the body into helping you change your mood.

3. Smiling Is Contagious
When someone is smiling they lighten up the room, change the moods of others, and make things happier. A smiling person brings happiness with them. Smile lots and you will draw people to you.

4. Smiling Relieves Stress
Stress can really show up in our faces. Smiling helps to prevent us from looking tired, worn down, and overwhelmed. When you are stressed, take time to put on a smile. The stress should be reduced and you'll be better able to take action.

5. Smiling Boosts Your Immune System
Smiling helps the immune system to work better. When you smile, immune function improves possibly because you are more relaxed. Prevent the flu and colds by smiling.

6. Smiling Lowers Your Blood Pressure
When you smile, there is a measurable reduction in your blood pressure. Give it a try if you have a blood pressure monitor at home. Sit for a few minutes, take a reading. Then smile for a minute and take another reading while still smiling. Do you notice a difference?

7. Smiling Releases Endorphins, Natural Pain Killers and Serotonin
Studies have shown that smiling releases endorphins, natural pain killers, and serotonin. Together these three make us feel good. Smiling is a natural drug.

8. Smiling Lifts the Face and Makes You Look Younger
The muscles we use to smile lift the face, making a person appear younger. Don't go for a face lift, just try smiling your way through the day -- you'll look younger and feel better.

9. Smiling Makes You Seem Successful
Smiling people appear more confident, are more likely to be promoted, and more likely to be approached. Put on a smile at meetings and appointments and people will react to you differently.

10. Smiling Helps You Stay Positive
Try this test: Smile. Now try to think of something negative without losing the smile. It's hard. When we smile our body is sending the rest of us a message that "Life is Good!" Stay away from depression, stress and worry by smiling.

3. Watch your 'self-talk'

We all talk to ourselves and it is very important what we say when doing so.

The best description I have come across is from *Lisa* Quast, President, Career Woman, Inc. which is as follows:-

When I think about self-talk I think of that interesting little voice in our heads we hear after certain situations that helps us evaluate and make sense of what has happened. This self-talk can be positive or negative, and, it can turn into a self-fulfilling prophecy.

For example, I often have people come to me for advice on how they can get a raise or promotion. Those who come to me with a positive attitude that they are worthy of obtaining a higher salary or promotion are much more likely to accomplish their goal because their self-talk is positive and it reinforces that they can figure out a way to make it happen (thus it becomes a self-fulfilling prophecy).

Those who come to me wanting to obtain a raise or promotion but have a negative attitude, an attitude in which they doubt they will ever get the raise or promotion they want because...and then proceed to list for me all the reasons why they don't believe it will happen, are engaging in negative self-talk. These are generally the people who don't end up getting that raise or promotion. Their negativity ends up surrounding them to such an extent that they become demotivated and don't want to go through the steps necessary to map out an action plan to accomplish their goal.

Positive self-talk is incredibly important because it helps to positively reinforce certain behaviours; behaviours that are necessary to self management. It has been my experience in coaching others that negative self-talk allows a person a reason to cut themselves slack, to be "off the hook" for their behaviour, for their lack of self management and thus of outcomes.

I have found that people with positive self-talk are much more willing to create a personal development plan for self-improvement and are better at managing and turning negative work situations into positive outcomes. I believe positive self-talk results in positive outcomes because it helps us control our behaviour and thus control our environment.

So, how about giving yourself a quick pat on the back and some encouraging words the next time you want to achieve a goal?

Try it for yourself and you just might be pleasantly surprised with the outcome!

For some more tips on positive thinking and collect a free eBook called

The Common Denominator of Success

Visit this site http://www.tips-on-positive-thinking.co.uk

4. Repeat your own Affirmations daily

This is something we all need to do to keep on track and to reach the goals we have set ourselves.

Some examples are:-
I am happy,
I am in good health,
I am fit and healthy
I can do this
I deserve to be great

You can find many more examples by searching on line, although only you know what it is you want!

Apart from repeating your affirmations it is also a good idea to write them down as well, thus reinforcing your intentions

Writing Affirmations

Writing affirmations this is a personal and powerful exercise. You first need to choose something that you would like to have in your life.

There are a number of things to keep in mind when creating your affirmations.

First off they all need to be in the present tense as if you already have achieved that which you wish

You also need to make them believable, and in the present tense.

The following notes are Courtesy of Think Right Now!
http://www.thinkrightnow.com

I also call affirmations self-instructions because that describes what they do. They instruct us how to feel and how to act. They affirm who we are at the deepest levels. They are the most powerful and the easiest tools to use for changing your emotions and the results you get in your life... If you use the right self-instructions. And use them A LOT.

You see, every moment of every day you are thinking. You can't stop it. Even if you are an experienced mediator, you would find it hard to turn off the pictures, sounds and feelings your mind serves up. Every minute of every day you are affirming what you already believe.
You are doing it this very second.

And in order to change your life, you must change your affirmations, your self-instructions... what you believe and accept as true.
If you doubt it, then you thought, *"That's not true."*

But guess what... That was an affirmation, too - a statement of belief and conviction.

In fact, every statement you've ever made or ever will make and every thought you've had or ever will have is a question, an affirmation or an affirmative command.

"Is that true?" (That's a question)

"Yes that's true," (That's an affirmation)

"Please leave," (affirmative command)

"I am not going anywhere!" (Affirmation)

"Sit down," (affirmative command)

"This is interesting," "I don't know," "This is boring," "I'm hungry," "I'm tired," "This is never going to work," "I feel incredible," "I can't concentrate," "This is easy," "Lifting weights is invigorating," "I hate sweating."

All just affirmations or you can call them Self-instructions.

So anyone that says affirmations don't work has absolutely no idea what they are talking about. Zero. Because they are 'working' on you right now and they will 'work' on you until you shuffle off these mortal coils.

What's my point? (Question)

Since your minute by minute affirmations (*thoughts*) represent your past, present and – most likely – your future beliefs and attitudes, if you elevate your affirmations toward what is most useful and empowering, you would enjoy greater success, better health and true peace of mind with very little effort.

For some more thoughts on the subject read chapter 11 on the subject of Remember the past is the past.

5. Never be late

Or should we say always be on time, as the brain does not recognize negatives.

I'm sure that none of us likes to be kept waiting, so let's behave as we would like to be treated and never be late for anything.

Time is a precious resource and should never be wasted, it is important that you let your friends and colleagues know that this is your view of life and unless you are relaxing or taking some time off always ensure you are using your time wisely as the moment you are in is all you have.

Should you feel the need to improve on your time management skills there are hundreds of books, CDs available to help you at very little cost.

A short list of titles can be found under resources and the end of this book, or you can just do a search on the Internet.

Avoid Being Late   By: David Korn

Being on time is one of the most important punctual aspects of life. It is important to avoid being late in order to not cause any problems. Learning how to be on time does take dedication and attention. There are several effective ways in adopting better time management techniques. Learning to be on time is definitely one of them.

A good way to avoid being late is to prepare ahead of time. For instance, you can prepare your items before you go to sleep the night before. Also, you can prepare batch amounts over the weekend or at times when things aren't so busy. By preparing ahead of time, you can save a lot of time and from being potentially late to an event. That way you can grab what you need as soon as you walk out of the door.

Setting reminders is a good way to be on time. Many of us use alarm clocks; wake up calls, portable device sounds, and so on as our reminders. The idea is to set these reminders ahead of time such that you don't forget. Having these reminders go off in a routine basis can be useful as well. Having a routinized reminder system can help you to easily remember the schedule. That way you can avoid being late on a daily basis.

Avoiding or eliminating distractions is important for being on time. Sometimes we get caught up in something prior to departure. It is a good idea to minimize these interruptions such that we can arrive at our destination on time. Good communication with others as well as learning to turn off or divert distracting items will be useful. That way you have a clear road ahead in order to arrive at your destination without being late.

Of course, one of the best ways to avoid being late is to leave early. After a while, you will be able to estimate how long it will take you to get to a destination. It is important to take into account any interruptions that normally occur on the way. That way you can leave early enough before any of this occurs.

Unfortunately, things come up in life which can prevent us from being on time. It can be understandable depending on the circumstance. Just as long as being late isn't a habit, many onetime circumstances can be excused.

Being late to an event can cause all sorts of problems. This can get one to be fired from a job, bad marks in school, cause upset in others, be seen as unreliable, and much more. Therefore, it is important to be on time to events.
Being on time will make you seem
Dependable,
Punctual,
Diligent.

These qualities are important for our personalities. When we arrive on time, we can feel at ease that we done our job.

6. Choose your company carefully – Mix with the right people

This is important as your company can and does influence your views.

We all need to be selective in choosing our friends as they can motivate us and encourage us if they are like us or they can de-motivate us and discourage us from achieving whatever it is we have set ourselves as a goal.

Good friends with the right attitude can help tremendously in overcoming the obstacles of life.

If you want to be successful, it is a good idea to hang out with successful people. It is said that birds of a feather flock together. Because it is very difficult to succeed by yourself

Be careful not to waste too much time with those who would drag you down, as you cannot get any more time, once it's spent it's spent and gone forever.

Successful people will always as a rule be prepared to help those who earnestly desire to be successful and are seeking advice.

As was said by Ben Franklin "The doors of wisdom are never shut"
According to *Jack Canfield*

"Self-esteem is a huge piece of my work. You have to believe it's possible and believe in yourself. Because after you've decided what you want, you have to believe it's possible and possible for you, not just for other people. Then you need to seek out models, mentors, and coaches."

A few other quotes from well known successful people

Dealing with people is probably the biggest problem you face, especially if you are in business. Yes, and that is also true if you are a housewife, architect or engineer.
Dale Carnegie

It's a fact that more people watch television and get their information that way than read books. I find new technology and new ways of communication very exciting and would like to do more in this field.
Stephen Covey

A pleasing personality helps you win friends and influence people. Add character to that formula and you keep those friends and maintain the influence.
Zig Ziglar

Never lose sight of the fact that the most important yardstick of your success will be how you treat other people
Barbara Bush

Seek out the best company you can and find the best teachers to help you and if you can find a great teacher you will find that they can inspire you to achieve great things.

It is said that we are a direct reflection of the five people we hang around the most, and our income is the average of those five people.

If you need to find the right people you can either join a group of like-minded people or join a brain-storming group – both groups can be found easily with an internet search or by just asking around.

One very good read is Dale Carnegie's
How to Win Friends and Influence People.

7. Laugh at yourself

We all need not to be too serious about ourselves.

According to William A Ward "A well-developed sense of humour is the pole that adds balance to your steps as you walk the tightrope of life"

The following 10 tips are Courtesy of www.goodtoknow.co.uk
by Rob Mansfield

'Laughter is the best medicine': we're always being told that, but there's actually more to a good giggle than just raising our spirits for a couple of minutes.

Research shows that while children laugh up to 400 times a day, adults do it only 17 times a day, on average.

In fact, laughter therapy is a big deal and can improve your health in lots of different ways. Just check out these 10 benefits of chuckling...

1. Laughter boosts your immune system

Researchers have found that laughter actually boosts the immune system, increasing the number of antibody-producing T cells. This then makes us less likely to get coughs and colds. It also lowers the levels of at least four hormones that are associated with stress, so after a good giggle you should be far less tense and anxious.

2. Laughter relieves pain

A good chortle has been found to reduce pain. Not only does it distract you from aches, but it releases feel good endorphins into your system that are more powerful than the same amount of morphine.

3. Laughter improves your social life

If you can make people laugh, then you're likely to have more friends, because everyone loves a joker. You're also likely to achieve more at work: if you have a good sense of humour you'll be more productive, a better communicator and team player.

In fact, most things we laugh at aren't necessarily actual jokes, but comments in everyday conversation. Laughter is as much about social relationships as it is about humour.

4. Laughter helps relieve depression

Laughter has long been known to help people who are suffering from the either SAD or full-blown depression. Laughing reduces tension and stress, and lowers anxiety and irritation, which are all major factors that contribute to the blues.

5. Laughter boosts your relationship

If you're looking to find a new partner, then laughter will help you find a new mate. Men love women who laugh in their presence and women actually laugh 125% more than men.

And if you're already with someone, then a shared sense of humour is an important factor in keeping your relationship running smoothly.

6. Laughter gives you a mini-work-out

We've probably all used, or at least heard, the phrase 'my sides ache' after laughing too much. Well, it's no real surprise. A good belly laugh exercises the diaphragm, contracts your abdominal muscles and also works your shoulders. This will make you feel a lot more relaxed.

In fact, laughing 100 times is the equivalent to 10 minutes on the rowing machine or 15minutes on an exercise bike, so break out those Only Fools And Horses DVDs and start watching!

7. Laughter protects your heart

According to a study by heart specialists at the University of Maryland, people with heart disease were 40% less likely to laugh in a variety of situations compared to people of the same age without heart disease.

Laughter has been found to benefit the way blood flows around the body, reducing the likelihood of heart disease. The research said that 15 minutes of laughter a day is as important for your heart as 30 minutes of exercise 3 times a week!

8. Laughter lowers your blood pressure

People who laugh a lot on a regular basis have lower blood pressure than the average person. When people have a good laugh, the blood pressure increases at first, but then it decreases to levels below normal.

Breathing then becomes deeper and this helps to send oxygen-rich blood and nutrients throughout the body.

9. Laughter improves your breathing

Laughter empties your lungs of more air than it takes in resulting in a cleansing effect - similar to deep breathing. This is especially helpful for people who are suffering from respiratory ailments, such as asthma.

10. Laughter helps you lose weight

Burning off calories by laughing might not sound as if it has much use, but a hearty chuckle raises the heart rate and speeds up the metabolism.

You have seen them.
You have watched them from afar.
You have even wanted to be more like them.

They are the **funny** and **charming** individuals who weave effortlessly through crowded galas, restaurants and events, making people smile and laugh, and always in demand at both business and social functions. They are never at a loss for associates, friends and lovers. They are the people that everyone wants to sit by, to talk to and to have around.

"These are the people who have developed their own unique sense of humour!"

Do you want to know why humour is so important?
Quite simply, humour makes other people happy. Why do you think that most people who fill out questionnaires about what they find attractive in a mate list "a sense of humour" as one of the top two most attractive features about a person? Because humour joins people together in a bond of camaraderie, emotion and trust! <u>Many people judge the physical appearance of funny people much higher than the physical appearance of dull people even if their actual looks are about the same!</u>

In addition, humour is <u>HEALTHY</u>! People who laugh have less stress, and less stress means fewer health problems!

8. Breathe deeply 3 times a day for 3 minutes

It is said that breathing properly helps reduce stress, which these days is something many people suffer from.

What's more it costs nothing to carry out a few breathing exercises except a few minutes of your time.

These exercises are very similar to those that help you laugh at yourself in that they are health related which is the most important thing in life to have – good health, as without it life becomes challenging to say the least.

Breathing correctly is not only important for living longer but also to have a good mood and keep performing at your best.

Here are 18 tips found on the Internet – with a link at the end to get your own tips directly in your inbox.

1. **Breathing Detoxifies and Releases Toxins**.
   Your body is designed to release 70% of its toxins through breathing. If you are not breathing effectively, you are not properly ridding your body of its toxins i.e. other systems in your body must work overtime which could eventually lead to illness. When you exhale air from your body you release carbon dioxide that has been passed through from your bloodstream into your lungs. Carbon dioxide is a natural waste of your body's metabolism.

2. **Breathing Releases Tension**
   Think how your body feels when you are tense, angry, scared or stressed. It constricts. Your muscles get tight and your breathing becomes shallow. When your breathing is shallow you are not getting the amount of oxygen that your body needs.

3. **Breathing Relaxes the Mind/Body and Brings Clarity**
   Oxygenation of the brain reducing excessive anxiety levels. Paying attention to your breathing. Breathe slowly, deeply and purposefully into your body. Notice any places that are tight and breathe into them. As you relax your body, you may find that the breathing brings clarity and insights to you as well.

4. **Breathing Relieves Emotional Problems**.

Breathing will help clear uneasy feelings out of your body.

5. **Breathing Relieves Pain**.

You may not realize its connection to how you think, feel and experience life. For example, what happens to your breathing when you anticipate pain? You probably hold your breath. Yet studies show that breathing into your pain helps to ease it.

6. **Breathing Massages Your Organs**

The movements of the diaphragm during the deep breathing exercise massages the stomach, small intestine, liver and pancreas. The upper movement of the diaphragm also massages the heart. When you inhale air your diaphragm descends and your abdomen will expand. By this action you massage vital organs and improve circulation in them. Controlled breathing also strengthens and tones your abdominal muscles.

7. **Breathing Increases Muscle**

Breathing is the oxygenation process to all of the cells in your body. With the supply of oxygen to the brain this increases the muscles in your body.

8. **Breathing Strengthens the Immune System**

Oxygen travels through your bloodstream by attaching to haemoglobin in your red blood cells. This in turn then enriches your body to metabolise nutrients and vitamins.

9. **Breathing Improves Posture**

Good breathing techniques over a sustained period of time will encourage good posture. Bad body posture will result of incorrect breathing so this is such an important process by getting your posture right from early on you will see great benefits.

10. **Breathing Improves Quality of the Blood**

Deep breathing removes all the carbon-dioxide and increases oxygen in the blood and thus increases blood quality.

11. Breathing Increases Digestion and Assimilation of food.
The digestive organ such as the stomach receives more oxygen, and hence operates more efficiently. The digestion is further enhanced by the fact that the food is oxygenated more.

12. Breathing Improves the Nervous System
The brain, spinal cord and nerves receive increased oxygenation and are more nourished. This improves the health of the whole body, since the nervous system communicates to all parts of the body.

13. Breathing Strengthen the Lungs.
As you breathe deeply the lung become healthy and powerful, a good insurance against respiratory problems.

14. Proper Breathing makes the Heart Stronger.
Breathing exercises reduce the workload on the heart in two ways. Firstly, deep breathing leads to more efficient lungs, which means more oxygen, is brought into contact with blood sent to the lungs by the heart. So, the heart doesn't have to work as hard to deliver oxygen to the tissues. Secondly, deep breathing leads to a greater pressure differential in the lungs, which leads to an increase in the circulation, thus resting the heart a little.

15. Proper Breathing assists in Weight Control.

If you are overweight, the extra oxygen burns up the excess fat more efficiently. If you are underweight, the extra oxygen feeds the starving tissues and glands.

16. Breathing Boosts Energy levels and Improves Stamina

17. Breathing Improves Cellular Regeneration

18. Breathing Elevates Moods.
Breathing increase pleasure-inducing neurochemicals in the brain to elevate moods and combat physical pain

How to breathe properly?
In order to breathe properly you need to breathe deeply into your abdomen not just your chest. Even in the old Greek and Roman times the doctors recommended deep breathing, the voluntary holding of air in the lungs, believing that this exercise cleansed the system of impurities and gave strength. This certainly is of great value to you in your work in the world. Breathing exercises should be deep, slow, rhythmic, and through the nose, not through the mouth. The most important parts of deep breathing has to be regulating your breaths three to four seconds in, and three to four seconds out.

1. Inhale through your nose, expanding your belly, then fill your chest. Counting to 5
2. Hold and Count to 3. Feel all your cells filled with golden, healing, balancing Sun light energy.
3. Exhale fully from slightly parted mouth and Feel all your cells releasing waste and emptying all old energy. Counting to 5.

Schedule your deep breathing exercise just as you would schedule important business appointments. Set aside a minimum of two 10 minute segments of time everyday although you can begin with two five minutes segments if you prefer.

Honouring yourself enough to schedule time with yourself is the first step in mastering stress. Tend to your relationship with yourself and your relationship with life and with others will be enriched and deepened accordingly. Remember to share with your children and all your friends and loved ones so that they too can reap its untold benefits.

Here is the link for your own messages direct to your inbox – I must point out that I have no connection with this organization and take no responsibility for the advice offered.

FREE Subscription - Click here to get articles like '18 Benefits of Deep Breathing and How to Breathe Deeply?' in your Email.

9. Walk for One Mile three times a week

Closely related to the previous chapter, all about exercise and the benefits we get from it.

This is one of the best ways to keep fit and healthy as walking is a natural thing to do.

Not only does this get you out in the fresh air it also helps your self-discipline which is important in all areas of life.

Walking is an ordinary everyday activity that nearly all of us take for granted. It is however an excellent and free natural exercise that can help you stay healthy and live longer, controls your weight.

Walking really is good exercise. And what is more Doctors agree that regular physical activity like walking helps protect the body from many illnesses and conditions, including heart disease and stroke, high blood pressure, osteoarthritis, obesity, the most common type of diabetes and many cancers.

It's also a great way to relieve stress and stay happy. Everyone knows how a good walk can help you collect your thoughts, and being outdoors, especially in green spaces, can help fight depression and improve mental health.

And the best news is – almost everyone can do it, anywhere and at any time, for free! You don't need special clothing, equipment or training, there are no gym memberships to pay, and it's so easy and natural there's very little risk you'll injure yourself.

Walking is especially convenient because it helps you do two things at once. While enjoying healthy physical activity, you could also be:

- Getting to places you need to visit, for example by walking to work, school or the shops.
- Spending time with others – friends, children and family. Walking and talking go hand in hand and you might even make new friends along the way.
- Exploring your local area – it's the best way to discover hidden corners up close.
- Enjoying green spaces and nature – fresh air, peace and a place for the kids to run around. …or just taking time to relax by yourself!

This information is courtesy of the following web site link.
http://www.getwalking.org/benefits-of-walking/benefits-of-walking/

Simple work-outs may trigger the release of neurochemicals known as endorphins. These chemicals are responsible for making us feel happy and by feeling happier; a more positive effect on the brain can be observed.

Just do simple exercises like a simple walk or jog. It may not be as intense as a full-blown work-out. You just have to keep your body physically fit and active.

10. Live in 'the Now' this very minute

As someone once said to me "when in the room – be in the room"
In other words pay attention be where you are- if at work don't spend your time thinking about home and if at home don't spend your time thinking about work.

All you have is now – you cannot live for the morrow or re-live yesterday so you might as well make the most of what you have today.

It is said that yesterday is gone forever and tomorrow is a promissory note so all you have is today – that is now.

Have you ever worked out that there are 1,440 minutes in a day – do you know how many you use wisely? Or how many you waste?

How to Live In the Now by Karim Hajee

The reason you have trouble living in the now is because your mind is simply not used to doing this. Your mind is used to remembering the past or worrying about the future - it can't live in the present because it doesn't know how. But you can teach your mind how to do this and I'm about to outline some simple steps that you can take to start living in the now.

First take a look at your present situation and ask yourself what's wrong with the very moment you are in. Don't think about what happened yesterday or sometime in the past. Don't focus on what might or might not happen tomorrow. Take a look at the very moment you are in not five minutes from now - and see if there is anything wrong. If you are at home - is there something wrong? Don't say you are out of work - that's not the present moment because you are looking at what is not happening. I want you to focus your mind on what is happening - then see what is wrong with that picture. My point is you should find nothing wrong with the present moment - it is what it is - and once you accept it - you can start living again.

Let's face it you can't turn your mind off - but you can get it to work differently and that's what you should start doing. Because if you don't take control of your mind your mind will control you - and that's not going to help you improve your life.

Ask yourself these next questions.

Do you find yourself waiting for something to happen?

Are you waiting to get some more time?

Make more money?

Meet the right person?

Are you waiting for the right opportunity?

Waiting is another game the mind plays because it doesn't want to live in the present moment. If you answered yes to any of the above questions then you are not living in the present moment - you are focusing on anything but the present moment. I know you can't focus on the present moment or live in the now 24 hours a day. But start by doing this for a few minutes a day and then continue expanding the exercise every day.

Then track your progress. See how you feel when you only focus on what is happening right now. As you continually do this you'll see yourself starting to enjoy the process.

Here's a suggestion. The next time you are driving or walking pay attention only to what is happening around you. Listen to the sounds, observe the people. Don't think about what you have to do or what happened yesterday or what might happen tomorrow or what might happen in five minutes.

Focus your attention only on what is happening right now. Doing this will get your mind to start living in the present moment and before you know it you'll be able to focus your mind and utilize the power of now.

http://www.creatingpower.com/index.html

11. Remember the past is the past

Whatever you did yesterday is gone forever – this habit is similar to the last one – all about living in the present.

You cannot undo whatever it is you think you made a mistake with you can only re-do it better today.

It's a great day to be alive. It's another day to learn.

Today is a day to give of you in labour.

Today is a day to play, to grow and to achieve your dreams... after all, you have dreams and you have but one life to achieve them.

Did you notice that? Those statements...
All of them are statements of belief - of conviction... of affirmation.

Even if you're already extremely skilled in some area of life, if you wanted to, you could enjoy even greater accomplishments by transforming your thoughts.

A large part of our research at Think Right Now International is to catalog and compare the beliefs, attitudes and actions of the world's most successful, happiest people to the most unsuccessful, unhappy people.

They are *always* polar opposites.

For example, when the healthiest, oldest living people on the planet feel comfortably full, they typically say to themselves, "I feel just right." And they stop eating even if a pile of their favourite food is still on their plates...

But what do people who suffer the most illnesses, pain and diseases do at the full mark? Yup. They often say things like, *"One more bite won't hurt," "It' so good, I can't stop," "Oh, it's small," "I'll just eat light tomorrow," "I'm still hungry," "I can't throw this good food away," "There's just a few bites left – might as well finish it."* And they continue eating.

In every discipline or area of life, we always find *hundreds* and often *over one thousand* differences in core belief and attitude patterns between successful people and those who routinely fail.

And the sobering truth is that the longer a person owns a belief (affirms it), the harder it is to change. The old saying that you can't teach old dog new tricks is an old saying for a good reason. Because our minds don't like change… it is uncomfortable to change.

You see, the pain you feel now might be bad, but at least it's familiar. You are handling it. But when big habit changes happen quickly, it's doubly agonizing because they are unfamiliar…unknown. And the unknown can be frightening.

That's why when you read a self-help book, go to therapy or to a seminar, chances are excellent that you will do nothing different. Or if you do experience an improvement in your moods or habits, it's usually very short lived. Why? Because you're long-held assumptions, beliefs and attitudes (lifelong affirmations) were never changed. You simply had a few more facts… So you unconsciously resist the change…

You found reasons why you couldn't continue, why you didn't like it, why it was wrong for you, why you couldn't succeed after all.

Because facts and logic alone are never enough with the biggest challenges of life.

If just knowing what to do guaranteed success, then everyone would get straight A's in school and would go on to have successful careers in their chosen field of study.

But they don't.

Out of every 100 students using the same text book, hearing the same lectures from the same teacher, only a few will score 90+ and even fewer will use their schooling to ensure success in career and life.

Because facts and logic alone are never enough.

Why? Because we are talk to ourselves all day long. In fact, our research found that most people's current thoughts (affirmations) are the same ones they had many years before. Most people have the same failure oriented beliefs in 2007 that they had in 1997, 1987 and 1977. If something frightened you 10 years ago, it's likely to still make your knees knock today. If you hate exercising now, you probably won't like it 10 years from now. And no matter how much gear you buy, you'll probably still affirm (believe) the same things about it that you do now. If you are a disorganized mess maker now, you'll probably be the same ten and twenty years from now.

Why is this so? I call it mental patterns. They are hard-wired into you from years of conditioning.

I have many clients whose core mental patterns are so disempowering, they suffer from panic attacks. They lose all control of their minds and bodies. But in most cases, when we aggressively work to alter their moment by moment thought which alters their core assumptions about themselves and about life, the 'disorder' called panic attack ends. This is true even if therapy has done nothing and the toxic psychoactive drugs they've been taking for decades have damaged their brains. Yup. Self-instructions *are* powerful.

Our research shows that without mental conditioning through massive repetition of positive opposing thought, the things you are bad at today you will still be bad at in ten years.

In most cases "Same sh*t, different day" is a cliché because, unfortunately, it's true for most people.

Think of your usual thoughts (affirmations) as a paint brush that continues to paint the same colours on the same places on the same canvas… for the rest of your life. The longer you paint, the thicker the paint gets. It gets so deep that there comes a point where it feels impossible to change the picture.

"Quitting smoking is so hard," "I'll never figure this out," "You make me so mad," "Everyone my age is overweight," "I'm just not good at this," "I'm not meant to have a lot of money," "I'm too busy to eat healthier," "I'll never get caught up," "I'm so depressed," "I feel like I'm going to die," "I knew it wasn't going to work," "I need some chocolate," "I'm so disorganized," "There are no decent men out there."

These kinds of beliefs (affirmations) fill you with anxiety. They make simple decisions difficult, suck the joy out of your accomplishments, create illness and disease, take away your energy and zest for adventure. In any area of life where you cannot seem to succeed no matter what, I guarantee you that beliefs like those above are controlling you every minute of every day.

But they don't have to any more.

Ponder this fact... Every sentence you've read here is a question, an affirmation or an affirmative command. Check it. Believe in affirmations now? Good. Step 1 is complete.

Now for Step 2. Pick any area of your life that doesn't work where you fail, feel fearful, hopeless or where your luck is never any good. It could be your poor diet, lack of fitness, anxiety/depression, career trouble, problems in the friendships/social arena, bad romances/sex, financial woes, poor organization, sports, study habits/test taking, memory, time management... any area of life where you are having big troubles or where you want to be a top performer.

Next, go somewhere by yourself and think about that topic. Notice your thoughts.

Whenever you notice a disempowered thought...one that makes you feel like crap, when you see a picture/movie of yourself failing or if you hear yourself say anything that makes you feel less capable, write down the thought or description of the pictures and feelings.

For example, if you want to improve your financial situation, you must get by yourself and listen to your inner dialog and notice your mental pictures about these issues. When you hear or see a rotten one, write it down. Then when you've done this for a while, take this list of problem beliefs/attitudes and write opposing statements in affirmation form.

So if you routinely get up late, don't start your daily phone calls until 11:00, take long lunches, spend money you shouldn't and never read investment related books or invest in appreciating assets, turn these beliefs, attitudes and actions around by writing down opposing first-person, present-tense statements of affirmation. These statements will command your mind to believe differently, to feel differently and to act differently.

Take this new set of desired beliefs, attitudes and actions and copy each one down on a sheet of paper and live with those cards. Take it everywhere with you and read them with strong emotion upon waking, at lunchtime and before you go to bed. Say them aloud whenever possible. Commit to doing this and soon you'll be taking positive daily action related to financial matters that are exactly like the best money-makers and money-managers alive.

If you think this won't have an incredibly positive effect on your emotions and your actions, remember that that belief/attitude is an affirmation.

Suspend the doubt and follow through on this and you will have taken the most important step in your personal and professional development. Do this and nothing will be beyond your grasp.

Your confidence will soar.

Your motivation will last.

Your follow through will be perfect.

Any goal will be possible for you.

Happiness will be your normal mental state.

Courtesy of Think Right Now! http://www.thinkrightnow.com

12. Believe in Yourself

Have Belief in Your Own Ability

Confidence is more than just the absence of doubt. It is the complete certainty in ability or of outcome.

It comes from previous success at a thing, from encouragement, intense desire, imagination, preparation and from courage... the ability to get yourself to do a thing even though you may be scared out of your mind.

Because confidence is not an absence of fear.

Confidence in your ability to do a thing won't absolutely guarantee your success, but it can help to keep you from quitting.

Confidence eliminates worry. It can help you enjoy yourself. And An *I Can* attitude will help you to visualize success more clearly.
There is no doubt that you can accomplish anything if you put your mind into it. The only problem is that many people do not know how to use their minds to their best advantage.

In the absence of experience, you must rely on faith and on your imagination.

That's where each book you read or CD you listen to you will hear powerful new ideas that you believe you can succeed no matter what the risks.

You'll hear that you are willing to do your best. You will hear that you are an I CAN type of person. You'll hear that there is no room for doubt, that you are filled with confidence and faith in your ability to succeed.
And with these powerful beliefs propelling your actions, your stress goes down, your mind works faster, solutions and ideas come to you easier, you'll ask better questions, get better answers, temptations are less tempting.

In short, you'll be able to tap into and use more of the talents and abilities you were blessed with when you were born.

If you do not believe in yourself how you can expect others to believe in you?

You will find a list or resources at the end of the book, all of them designed to help you achieve whatever it is you seek to obtain.

13. Visualize Your Goals daily

Visualization – said to be a very important ingredient in reaching your goals in life.

As Napoleon Hill said in his famous book "Think and Grow Rich" whatever the mind of man can conceive and believe he can achieve

Once you know what I is you want to achieve you just need to close your eyes and visualize it – make it real – add colour – add sound – be the Director of your own movie.

Research suggests that those who practice the art of visualization achieve better and greater results over those who do not.

If you practice imagining your results on a daily basis this re-enforces your desire to achieve and the sub-conscious goes to work to bring about the result your are looking for.

Visualization has helped many people achieve their goals. And it can be a most powerful tool. For It gives you the power to identify the obliterate roadblocks to progress.

It makes your path to success so real that you can almost feel it, hear it, smell it, as well as see it in the mind's eye.

People who have benefited from using visualization come from all walks of life. From salespeople to managers all who have continued to improve year on year. And from athletes whose championship dreams have come true.

There are many benefits of visualization—so why not start to use this powerful method to achieve your goals today.

I believe that all top achievers use visualization to increase their chances of success in whatever they are endeavouring to achieve at that moment in their lives.

It must be said like anything other tool it needs to be practised on a regular basis in order to see any results.

What is goal visualization?
Goal visualization is nothing but imagining yourself as a person with all your dreams fulfilled. If your goal is to have a dream house then visualize it. Visualize yourself in that house. If you feel good about it and are sure that it the house you want, it will inspire you.

It will push you to achieve your goals. Never let go of that image and work towards making it a reality.

It's not dreaming
Goal visualization is not dreaming. What you dream is what your mind makes you dream. Visualization is what you want to dream. More importantly, goal visualization is not an involuntary action which is left entirely to your subconscious mind while you are asleep.

You have complete control over it and can think about it at your discretion. You have to create a clear picture of your goal.

Imagine yourself when you are older, living in your dream house, with your family.

An image like this will help you to achieve the goal by keeping you focused.

A good CD to listen to is "The Power of Visualization" by Lee Pulos

14. Play a CD instead of listening to the radio

When I say play a CD I do not mean a music CD but a motivational and inspirational one from someone who has achieved success in their chosen field.

These days one no longer has to be at home to listen to such inspiration as with the advent of technology you can listen while you walk, are on a train or in your car.

The choice of your favourite leader – speaker is very wide and the cost of either a CD or tape is inexpensive.

With repetition before long you find that your thinking has altered course and you are less distracted away from your goals.

A range of titles can be found under resources at the end of the book.

Some of us learn by reading, others listening, some by watching the idea of listening is that it can be done along with other activities; it is where you can turn your car into a mobile classroom, since you are travelling somewhere you might as well put the time to good use.

Nearly all successful people you will find have this sort of habit.

Life is full of unpleasant surprises and setbacks, so it's important to get a dose of inspiration on a regular basis

Why not make listening to *motivational CD's,* part of your daily routine.

Here are 14 great motivational quotes, from well known successful people, all who have produced recordings for you to listen to.

1. "You are the only real obstacle in your path to a fulfilling life."
Les Brown

2. "Don't wish it was easier, wish you were better. Don't wish for less problems, wish for more skills. Don't wish for less challenges, wish for more wisdom."
Jim Rohn

3. "To lead others is to help them change their thoughts, beliefs and actions for the better."
Jim Rohn

4. "Leaders aren't born, they are made. And they are made just like anything else, through hard work."
Vince Lombardi

5. "You can have everything in life you want if you will just help enough people get what they want".
Zig Ziglar

6. "It is literally true that you can succeed best and quickest by helping others to succeed."
Napoleon Hill

7. "You are the only real obstacle in your path to a fulfilling life."
Les Brown

8. "It's not whether you get knocked down; it's whether you get up."
Vince Lombardi

9. "You don't have to be great to get started, but you have to get started to be great."
Les Brown

10. "Though no one can go back and make a brand new start, anyone can start from now and make a brand new ending."
Author Unknown

11. "If you want to have more, you first have to become more."
Jim Rohn

12. "Without a sense of urgency, desire loses its value."
Jim Rohn

13. "The major reason for setting a goal is for what it makes of you to accomplish it. What it makes of you will always be far greater value than what you get."
Jim Rohn

14. "It is the set of sails, not the direction of the winds that determines which way we will go."
Napoleon Hill

15. Read motivational/inspirational books every day

Why should this be a daily habit – quite simply it is as Zig Ziglar would say no different from bathing – you need to do it daily otherwise there is no benefit to it.

Research has found that many people never pick up a book after they have left their formal education – however this is not the case with any successful person.

Jim Rohn would say that a home without books is like a house without windows.

Successful people have a library of books, not just one or two but whole bookcases full; they also will re-read many of them more than once just to remind themselves of the messages contained in them.

Here it is recommended that you follow the suggestions in the previous chapter where you will have found listed some great quotes from successful people who are also authors.

Reading will give you many ideas that can all help you achieve your various goals – it broadens the mind and gives you a blueprint from which to build your life, particularly if you read books from the past from great authors even as far back as Aristotle.

Today there is so much to choose from it is not always easy to decide what is best to read, however its well to remember that you cannot manufacture antiques, in other words there's no new wisdom just a different slant put on it; therefore you cannot go far wrong by reading the older titles from authors long passed away.

You can find a recommended list at the end of the book – various titles providing tips and ideas from successful people who have left clues about their success for our benefit.

For a free eBook **"The Common Denominator of Success"**

By Albert E.N. Gray

Visit http://www.tips-on-positive-thinking.co.uk/

16. Go the Extra mile

An important principle of success in all walks of life and in all occupations is a willingness to " Go The Extra Mile "; which means the rendering of more and better service than that for which one is paid, and giving it in a positive mental attitude. Search wherever you will for a single sound argument against this principle and you will not find it, nor will you find a single instance of enduring success, which was not attained in part by its application.

The principle is not the creation of man. It is a part of Nature's handiwork, for it is obvious that every living creature below the intelligence of man is forced to apply the principle in order to survive. Man may disregard the principle if he chooses, but he cannot do so and at the same time enjoy the fruits of enduring success.

The advantages of the habit of going the extra mile are definite and understandable. Let me examine some of them and be convinced. The habit brings the individual to the favourable attention of those who can and will provide opportunities for self-advancement.

It tends to make one indispensable, in many different human relationships and it therefore enables him to command more than average compensation for personal services. It leads to mental growth and to physical skill and perfection in many forms of endeavour; thereby adding to one's earning capacity. It protects one against the loss of employment when employment is scarce and places him in a position to command the choicest jobs.

It enables one to profit by the law of contrast since the majority of people do not practice the habit. It leads to the development of a positive, pleasing mental attitude, which is essential for enduring success. It tends to develop a keen, alert imagination because it is a habit, which inspires one continuously to seek new and better ways of rendering service. It develops the important quality of personal initiative. It develops self-reliance and courage.

It serves to build the confidence of others in one's integrity. It aids the mastery of the destructive habit of procrastination. It develops definiteness of purpose, insuring one against the common habit of aimlessness.

There is still another and a greater reason for following the habit of going the extra mile. It gives one the only logical reason for asking for increased compensation. If a man performs no more service than that for which he is being paid, then obviously he is receiving all the pay to which he is entitled.

He must render as much service as that for which he is being paid, in order to hold his job, or to maintain his source of income, regardless of how he earns it. But he has the privilege always of rendering an "over plus" of service as a means of accumulating a reserve credit of goodwill, and to provide a just reason for demanding more pay, a better position, or both.

In America, anyone may earn a living without the habit of going the extra mile. And many do just that, but the economic security and luxuries available under the great American way of life are available only to the individual who makes this principle a part of his philosophy of life and lives by it as a matter of daily habit.

Every known rule of logic and common sense forces one to accept this as true. And even a cursory analysis of men in the higher brackets of success will prove that it is true. It is a well-known fact that Andrew Carnegie developed more successful leaders of industry than has any other great American industrialist.

Most of them came up from the ranks of ordinary day labourers and many of them accumulated personal fortunes of vast amounts, more than they could acquire without the guidance of Mr. Carnegie. The first test that Mr.

Carnegie applied to any worker whom he desired to promote was that of determining to what extent the worker was willing to go the extra mile. It was this test that led to the discovery of Charles M Schwab.

Mr. Schwab first came to Mr. Carnegie's attention when he was working as a labourer in one of the steel master's plants. Close observation revealed that Mr. Schwab always performed more and better service than that for which he was paid. Moreover, he performed it with a pleasing mental attitude, which made him popular among his fellow workers. He was promoted from one job to another until at long last in 1901 he was made president of the great United States Steel Corporation at a salary of $75,000 a year.

Not through all the ingenuity of man, or all the schemes that men resort to in order to get something for nothing, could Charles M Schwab, the day labourer, have earned as much as $75,000 during his entire lifetime if he had not willingly adopted and followed the habit of going the extra mile.

On some occasions Mr. Carnegie not only paid Mr. Schwab's salary, which was generous enough, but he gave him as much as $1,000,000 as a bonus in addition to his regular salary. When Mr. Carnegie was asked why he gave Mr. Schwab a bonus so much greater than his salary, he replied in words that every worker, regardless of his job or wages, might well ponder. "I gave him his salary for the work he actually performed", said Mr. Carnegie, "and the bonus for his willingness to go the extra mile", thus setting a fine example to his fellow workers".

Think of that! A salary of $75,000 a year paid to a man who started as a day labourer and a bonus of more than ten times that amount for a good disposition expressed by a willingness to do more than he was paid for.

Verily it pays to go the extra mile, for every time an individual does so he places someone else under obligation to him. No one is compelled to follow the habit of going the extra mile, and seldom is anyone ever requested to render more service than that for which he is paid.

Therefore, if the habit is followed it must be adopted on one's own initiative.

There is still another benefit to be gained by the man who follows the habit of going the extra mile: It keeps him on good terms with his own conscience and serves as a stimulant to his own soul! Therefore, it is a builder of sound character, which has no equal in any other human habit.

The philosophy of Andrew Carnegie is essentially a philosophy of economics. But it is more than that! It is also a philosophy of ethics and sympathy for the weak and the unfortunate. It teaches one how to become his brother's keeper and at the same time rewards him for so doing.

The attitude of the man who follows the habit of going the extra mile is this. He recognises the truth that he is receiving pay for schooling himself for a better position and greater pay!

It was this very asset which enabled Charles M Schwab to climb, step by step, from the lowly beginning as a day labourer to the highest position his employee had to offer and it was this asset as well which brought Mr.Schwab a bonus of more than ten times the amount of his salary.

The million dollar bonus which Mr. Schwab received was his payoff for having put his best efforts into every job he performed - a circumstance that could not have happened if he had not followed the habit of going the extra mile.

Mr. Carnegie had but little, if anything, to do with the circumstance. It was entirely out of his hands. Let us be generous by assuming that Mr. Carnegie paid off because he knew Mr. Schwab had earned the additional pay, which had not been promised him. But the actual fact may be that he paid off rather than lose so valuable a man. And here let us note that the man who follows the habit of going the extra mile thereby places the purchaser of his services under a double obligation to pay a just compensation. On being an obligation based upon his sense of fairness, the other based on his sense of fear of losing a valuable man.

Thus we see that no matter how we view the principle of going the extra mile, we come always to the same answer, that it pays "compound interest" to all that follow the habit.

17. Act as if you are at where you wish to be

There's nothing you cannot do

There's nothing to fear, you're as good as the best.
As strong as the mightiest, too.
You can win in every battle or test.
For there's no one just like you.

There's only one you in the world today.
So nobody else, you see.
Can do your work in as fine a way.
You're the only you there'll be.

So face the world, and all life is yours.
To conquer and love and live.
And you'll find the happiness that endures.
In just the measure you give.

There's nothing too good for you to possess.
Nor heights where you cannot go.
Your power is more than belief or guess.
It is something you have to know.

There is nothing to fear, you can and you will.
For you are the invincible you.
Set your foot on the highest hill.
There's nothing you cannot do.

Author Unknown

My A B C is
Always
Believe You
Can
Do it

All you really need is what is called a burning desire – a must achieve reason.

For if the promise is clear the price is easy.

18. Tell your partner or a family member you Love them

No strings attached

I've nothing else to offer, so, to you, its love I'll send.
It's nothing that I borrowed and it's nothing that I'd lend.

It has no dollar value and it can't be overused.
It isn't fragile, so it can't break, though often it's abused.

I've given it to others, but each time it's unique.
Its meaning's always different; it depends on what you seek.

It's something you can store away, to feel when you're in need.
But never is it on display, its beauty can't be seen.

I'm giving it 'no strings attached,' no costly warranty.
This love that I am sending has a lifetime guarantee.

       Author Unknown

Three little words

One day a woman's husband died, and on that clear, cold morning, in the warmth of their bedroom, the wife was struck with the pain of learning that sometimes there isn't anymore.

No more hugs, no more special moments to celebrate together, no more phone calls just to chat, no more 'just one minute.'

Sometimes, what we care about the most gets all used up and goes away, never to return before we can say good-bye, or that we can say 'I love you."

So while we have it, it's best we love it, care for it, fix it when it's broken and heal it when it's sick. This is true for marriage, for old cars, for children with bad report cards, for dogs with bad hips and for aging parents and grandparents.

We keep them because they are worth it. Because we are worth it.

Some things we keep like a best friend who moved away or a classmate we grew up with. There are just some things that make us happy, no matter what. Life is important, like people we know who are special. And so, we keep them close!

It is important to let every one of our friends and family know that we love them, even if we think they don't love us back.

We would be amazed at what a smile and the three little words - 'I Love You' - can do.

Author Unknown

Another short poem: I May Never See Tomorrow

>I may never see tomorrow; there's no written guarantee,
>And things that happened yesterday belong to history,
>I cannot predict the future, I cannot change the past,
>I have just the present moment, I must treat it as my last,
>
>I must use this moment wisely for it soon will pass away,
>and be lost to me forever as part of yesterday,
>I must exercise compassion, help the fallen to their feet,
>Be a friend unto the friendless, make an empty life complete,
>
>The unkind things I do today may never be undone,
>And friendships that I fail to win may never more be won,
>I may not have another chance on bended knee to pray,
>And thank God with humble heart for giving me this day.
>
>Author Unknown

19. Carry out random acts of kindness for strangers

This does not mean any particular expense although you can if you wish – why not when using a Toll Road or Bridge pay the attendant for the people in the next car even when you have no idea who they are and if possible watch for the expression on their face.

Something we can all give is a Smile -

"A smile costs nothing, but gives much.

It enriches those who receive, without making poorer those who give.

It takes but a moment, but the memory of it sometimes lasts forever.

None is so rich or mighty that they can get along without it, and none is so poor, that they can be made rich by it.

A smile creates happiness in the home, fosters good will in business and is the countersign of friendship.

It brings rest to the weary, cheer to the discouraged, sunshine to the sad and it is nature's best antidote for trouble.

Yet it cannot be bought, begged, borrowed or stolen - for it is something that is of no value to anyone, until it is given away.

Some people are too tired to give you a smile.

Give them one of yours, as no one needs a smile so much as those who have no more to give."

Author Unknown

20. Watch One hour less television every day

Instead watch an inspirational DVD the choice these days is greater than ever.

You will find a few suggestions under the resources page at the end of this book.

Apart from those listed a number of other films worth watching are ones like – The Gladiator with Russell Crow, Schindler's list, Ben-Hur and The Colour Purple – why these you ask – simply because although entertaining they also contain worthwhile truths.

Studies have also found that watching too much television is bad for your health.

"People who spend more than four hours in front of the television each day have a far higher risk of dying early than those who limit their viewing, an Australian study reported in 2010.

Watching the small screen for prolonged periods is also bad for your heart, according to the research published in the *Journal of the American Heart Association*.

"Compared to people who watch less than two hours of television per day, people who watch more than four hours per day have a 46 percent higher risk of death from all causes," researcher David Dunstan told AFP.

They also have an 80 percent increased risk from cardiovascular disease, he said.

Sitting down for long periods stops the body from using its muscles and adequately processing sugars and fats, Dunstan said.

The findings come from a six-year study into the viewing habits of some 8,800 Australians which stripped out the influence of other health factors such as age, sex, smoking, weight and exercise".

In 2004 the BBC (British Broadcasting Corporation) said

Watching TV 'is bad for children'

Children under two should not be allowed to watch

any TV, experts say.

Older children should watch no more than two hours a day, the researchers at the Children's Hospital and Regional Medical Centre in Seattle said.

Each hour in front of the TV increased a child's chances of attention deficit disorder by 10%, their research in the Paediatrics journal showed.

The study of 1,345 children showed three hours TV a day made children 30% more likely to have the disorder.

Dr Dimitri Christakis at the children's hospital led the study. He said: "The newborn brain develops very rapidly during the first two to three years of life. It's really being wired."

Children who were exposed to the unrealistic levels of stimulation at a young age continued to expect this in later life, leading to difficulty dealing with the slower pace of school and homework, he said.

"TV can cause the developing mind to experience unnatural levels of stimulation," he said.

This was made worse by the rapid image change that television makers used to keep young children interested, Dr Christakis added.

Parents were questioned about their children's viewing habits and asked to rate their behaviour at age seven on a scale similar to that used to diagnose attention deficit disorders.

The youngsters who watched the most television were more likely to rank within the top 10% for concentration problems, impulsiveness, restlessness and being easily confused.

Frederick Zimmerman of the University of Washington in Seattle, another of the authors, said it was impossible to say what a "safe" level of TV viewing would be for children between the ages of one and three.

"Each hour has an additional risk. You might say there's no safe level since there's a small but increased risk with each hour," he said.

"Things are a trade-off. Some parents might want to take that risk. We didn't find a safe level in that sense."

Between three and five per cent of children in the US are diagnosed with attention deficit disorder.

The researchers admitted there could be problems in the study as the parents' views may not be totally accurate.

Also it was not possible to know whether the children already had attention problems early on that attracted them to TV viewing.

21. Be courteous to all

In other words Do as you would be done by for remember every action begets a reaction.

Exercise care because it is said when climbing the ladder of life treat the people you meet on the way with kindness as you may well meet them again if your progress ends and you find yourself back at the bottom of the ladder passing them on the way – and if you have treated those individuals badly I'm sure they will have remembered that.

This book is all about having good habits to improve life

Did you know that habits are incredibly powerful tools for personal growth and success?

Let's look a little closer at the meaning of the word habit.

Random House dictionary defines habit in this way:

Habit: An acquired behaviour pattern regularly followed until it becomes almost involuntary.

The important words in this definition are acquired and almost involuntary. Let me ask you a question. When is the last time you sat down and said to yourself?

"Today I am going to add a new habit to my life?"

I guess that you have probably never said those words.

What is a positive habit?

A positive habit is simply a habit that produces positive benefits, actions and attitudes you want to acquire and make part of your life. Why is there such great power in positive habits to effect change? Because habits; by their very nature, are automatic.

After a period of time they can become permanent.

So how do we go about adding new positive habit's to our life?

It's really quite simple.

You simply begin repeating an action, attitude or thought process every day for at least 21 days.

Research has shown that an action that is repeated for a minimum of 21 days is likely to become a habit.

Remember that positive habits have positive benefits and you will reap those benefits for as long as you maintain that habit.

Brian Tracy states the Law of Habit as: -

"In the absence of a specific decision on your part to change some aspect of your life, the natural tendency will be to go on the same way indefinitely. Ninety-five percent of what we do is habit."

You can create a new habit by just repeating an activity over and over again for approximately 21 days

The question to ask yourself is will I endeavour to put into practice some if not all of these 21 habits detailed in this book?

Conclusion

As with all good habits they are easy to do but also easy not to do.

You owe it to yourself to maintain good habits for you health and wellbeing if nothing else.

I'm sure you realise that habits are very powerful and affect every aspect of your life.

As has been said Habits become character – and character becomes destiny – where do you want to end up?

Remember it only takes 21 days to acquire a new habit and a new habit can replace an old habit and a new habit can transform your life.

Author: Alan Searing
Alan was born 1943 lives in Hertfordshire in U K.

Since age of 20 has always been self-employed and run his own businesses in various sectors, although primarily in retail.
Has an interest in personal development and has authored and published an eBook on Creating Better Habits in order to Live a Better Life, has also a CD of 21 good habits, which is available on eBay.

http://bit.ly/w6fLRh

In 2011 authored a new book "The Art of Growing Tomatoes" a comprehensive guide covering where to begin to using seeds or plants and all the ways you can grow tomatoes even without a garden.

Copyright 2012 and Published by Solutions4U Hoddesdon EN11 8DN UK

Other titles available

Creating Better Habits – How to Live a Better Life   http://amzn.to/wnis5n

The Art of Growing Tomatoes – with lots of tips   http://amzn.to/ysIy1J

Resources

Recommended reading, listening and watching:

Books
The Richest Man in Babylon by George S Clason
The Power of Positive Thinking – Norman Vincent Peale
You Can if You Think You Can – Norman Vincent Peale
The Power of Discipline – Brian Tracy
The Life you were Born to Live – Dan Millman
Success is a Journey – Brian Tracy
Think and Grow Rich – Napoleon Hill
As a Man Thinketh – James Allen
The Slight Edge by Jeff Olson
The Seasons of Life by Jim Rohn

CDs
Goals, How to set them, How to reach them – by Zig Ziglar
The Psychology of Winning by Denis Waitley
How to Master your Time by Brian Tracy
The Art of Exceptional Living by Jim Rohn
The Power of Visualization – by Lee Pulos
The Challenge to Succeed by Jim Rohn
The Psychology of Selling by Brian Tracy
The Strangest Secret by Earl Nightingale
The Seeds of Greatness by Denis Waitley
The Psychology of Achievement by Brian Tracy

DVDs
How to have your best year ever by Jim Rohn
Living an Exceptional Life by Jim Rohn
Secrets of Self-Made Millionaires by Brian Tracy
Step into your Greatness by Les Brown
The Success Principles by Jack Canfield
Winning – it's all in your head by Denis Waitley
The Secret by Rhonda Bryne
The Seven Habits of Highly Effective People by Stephen Covey
The 8th Habit by Stephen Covey
The Shift by Wayne Dyer

Made in the USA
Charleston, SC
27 June 2012